BOOKS OF DISCOVERY

– MY BOOK OF MIRACLES AND MAGIC –
NUMBER 3

THE TREASURY OF ANCIENT WISDOM

This book contains carefully compiled daily lessons and are to be practiced as part of a daily routine. You are advised not to move on to the next step, unless you have absorbed the day's lesson and it has become part of your daily habit. Avoid the temptation to skim through, or skip, parts of these lessons. It is only by consistent and applied practice that you will achieve sustainable results.

In the printed version the blank pages have been left for the reader to write their own notes and observations.

CONTENTS

PROLOGUE

This is the third book in the series My Book of Discovery. This book contains 92 daily lessons, using Ancient Wisdom to transform your life. In this book, deeper information and rituals are recorded, in order to utilise the knowledge of the Initiates as part of our daily life.

We recommend that the first two books in the series are completed before attempting to enter into the lessons contained in this book. This is because it is vital to have achieved a discipline, which has become seamless, and to have achieved a natural process, in the practise of ordering and selecting our thoughts and feelings.

Devoted daily practise is the key to success.

Welcome to the third book of discovery.

BLOCK OF LESSONS

Mornings are vital

DAY 1

Awaken with Security

To have arrived at this lesson, you will have already experienced how vital it is to your well- being, that you prepare your day from the moment you open your eyes.

Begin your morning by truly feeling the place in which you wake. Your physical sense of touch is how you commune with the Earth, the wonderful source of all that you have been given in the physical world. Each and every day is pristine and new. We have the chance to create whatever we want and it starts by how you greet the day. Let us make the decision to bring encouragement and joy to others throughout the day. Let us be grateful for the chance to begin this day anew.

Feel, that just for these few seconds, you are safe; you are secure. Dwell in the feeling of safety, so that you may draw to yourself, more of these experiences of security and peace.

DAY 2
Prepare the way you see the world

As we wash our hands, let us think of cleansing our vision of the world in which we live. Let us wash with care, our hands, our foreheads and the Ajna Chakra, so we may see with clarity, beyond the every- day assumptions and worldly cares.

Let us wash, with reverence, the Crown Chara and the back of the neck, so we may commune with sacred entities and walk carefully upon the Earth.

DAY 3

The Sun

Let us greet the Sun and the essence of daylight itself. Let give thanks for this fraction of a moment, that we shall never see again, before we let it go into the realms of memory.

Let us breathe in light itself and hold on to each breath, that its vitality shall never leave us.

If we truly wish to understand the source of life itself and to experience the world of light, then we have the greatest of all resources, the sun, and daylight itself. We must begin to love and appreciate physical light, if we ever want to truly understand higher realms of existence. Physical light is a living spirit and the source of all creation.

Let us join in a few moments of prayer and celebration, so that all we may touch the blessed.

DAY 4

The breathing technique of using the Ida and Pingala forces

The breathing technique of using the Ida and Pingala forces. We may now practise the method of activating the two forces of the sun and the moon. These two forces are, in fact, the one force of life itself, in their emissive and receptive states. These may be called masculine and feminine forces, and are represented by the sun and the moon.
This is one force, that flows down through the spinal cord, crossing and looping itself, as it descends.

This is illustrated by the symbol of Hermes Trismegitus, the winged wand. It has become used as the symbol of health, and may be even be seen outside chemist shops. Sometimes the life force is illustrated by a serpent entwining itself around a staff.

This technique requires practise.
Firstly, using the middle finger of your hand, press gently against the left nostril, so that it is blocked. Breathe in the light of the sun, or the daylight itself, through the right nostril. Hold the breath for as long as is comfortable. Switch to blocking the right nostril, using the same finger, and breathe out through the left nostril. Now breathe in through the left nostril, hold the light within, and breathe out through the right nostril.

This must be practised very gently and with reverence.

The right-side communes with the force of the sun and the emissive forces, and the left with the moon and the receptive forces. They are both aspects of the one force that descends the spinal cord and loops around at the base of spine, and ascends, once more to the source of life itself.

The spinal cord, is illustrated by the Palm Branch, which shows us the dorsal and cervical ganglia branching from the central cord, illustrated by the fronds of the palm. The Kundalini force lies dormant at the base of the spinal cord.

It is effective to use a simple, well known prayer, or one that you create yourself, whilst doing this. Breathe in the lines of the prayer that you wish to activate within yourself. Hold within, the words that you wish to work within you and then breathe out the words you wish to manifest upon the Earth.

DAY 5

Awakening Early

It is imperative that we wake early and carry out our daily techniques with care and respect. Learn to become part of the natural rhythm of life.

Developing these habits is vital to creating the life we wish to experience. The more care and discipline we put into the preparation of the day, the more we can take responsibility for the day's events and how we choose to react. Each act we carry out has its own important role.

Washing with great care is an ancient way of blessing and making sacred the day, which is about to unfold. Hold your hand for a short while under running water, consciously ask for the water to be consecrated and then use it gently and in silence as you wash. Even cleaning your teeth is a hugely important exercise. As you clean your teeth, remind yourself to clean away any unhelpful words and make a simple promise to speak words of kindness throughout the day.

Take a few moments to observe the extraordinary quintessence that radiates from the petals of a flower, just before the sun is breaking. Nothing is more luminous and crackling with magic and life!

DAY 6
Sacred silence

A day devoted to silence is of great benefit toward understanding the power of words. Choose a day when this may be possible. Spend a day in silence and learn to listen to the world around you. Words are a magic power, that travel far into the universe, way beyond our comprehension. By deciding to remain silent, even for one day, we may discover the immensity of the words that we spend so freely.

DAY 7

Weekly Reflection

Reflect on the week and how it has been used. What have you learned? What are the results of your actions and words?

Use this day as a day of reflection, prayer and gratitude. Call on all entities and forces to join with you in celebration of life and the creator of all.

BLOCK OF LESSONS

Valuing the night

DAY 8

Preparation for sleep

As we have learned, preparing for sleep is of paramount importance. Never go to bed without washing your feet! Do not forget that everything you have encountered, as you make your way through the world during the day, is absorbed through your feet. Even if your physical feet do not touch the ground, even if they are missing, you still have so many layers of etheric bodies! Wash your feet with care and respect, even in your mind's eye. Think about the places you may have ventured and the energies that you may have absorbed. Wash them away, purify yourself and allow the traces to gently diminish into the water. In this way we can approach the world of sleep, which is vast, with respect and clarity.

DAY 9
Decide

Always bless your body in the ways that we have already discovered. Always visualise a bright, shining light, like the sun, above you, just before you go to sleep. Always ask to be taken to the light in your sleep state. Ask to be admitted there to find your solutions, to greet loved ones, to receive any help you may need. Never, ever forget to go to the light in order to give thanks for life and all its blessings.

DAY 10
Love the dark

We often lapse into dividing the light and the dark. One is good and the other bad and full of evil intent; this is, of course, untrue. This fear of the dark has its origins in a primeval past, when all manner of danger lurked far from the safety of the firelight.

The night is very rarely, completely dark. The light of the sun is reflected by the stars and the moon. The moon teaches how to offer up our darkness to the light of the sun. This silver light is of a quintessence so pure, that nothing can be so poignant.

Dark entities

There is no battle between the forces of good and evil. Dark entities are carrying out with diligence their allotted tasks. It is only our human perception that is bound up in moral judgement. We do not take it upon ourselves to judge the fungi that create vast networks of communication beneath the earth. Nor do we decide that the vast tree roots are evil, or the insects that burrow deep within the earth are set out to do us wrong! The great and only Law of Eternal Life flows through all of creation; each must behave according to its nature.

Rather than wage yet another misguided war against the dark, it is better for us to learn all we can from the Living Book of Nature, and adapt ourselves to attracting what we feel is more beneficial to our lives and to the world in which we wish to live.

DAY 12

Stop!

We must stop searching out all manner of wrong doing and sniffing out the imagined perpetrators! We must concentrate, instead, upon our own business! That divine and infinite business of getting closer and closer to the very best and "real" version of ourselves that is forever awaiting us in Sephira Tifaret, in the heart of the sacred Tree of Life.

This is our only true sanctuary and our only true defence against our folly. When we truly begin to create this divine armoury, then there is nothing that can ever endanger us again.

Respect

How do we better encounter the forces of darkness? First and foremost, with respect. We must respect their role and their right to life. By acknowledging this, we soon find that these forces are prepared to negotiate. We cannot expect to win a war that does not exist with a bell, book and candle! By bellowing out commands in the name of the cross!

Neither is it fair to banish anything and send it packing; for where will it go? Whose lives will it persecute next? No, unless we truly understand the law and know exactly what words to use and where best to send the unfortunate being, then it is best not interfered with, at all!

All things live within the creator and within creation, each has its role to play. There is only the Creator and Creation! There are no wars, no conquests, no fights for supremacy against the Supreme Creator!

DAY 14

Weekly Review

So, are we ready to forgo our childish views of good and evil?
Are we ready to grow up, finally?
Are we prepared to do all it takes?
Are we ready to stop fuelling fires and to withdraw our energy for any cause other than that of becoming the world for which we wish?

BLOCK OF LESSONS

3

Consecration

DAY 15

A simple consecration for water

Firstly, choose a small bowl or cup and carefully clean it. Watch the water flow, before filling it. Hold your right hand under the water and say a few words of thanks. Fill the bowl with water.

Put the first two fingers of your right hand into the water. These two fingers are used because the forefinger is our connection with the Spirit and our own will. The second finger connects to the planet Mercury and the forces of communication.

Trace a circle three times, in a clockwise direction in the water, using these two fingers. Call upon the immense thought force of the Arch Angel of Water, Tsaphkiel, which means The Contemplation of the Creator. Ask this force to join you and move through you to consecrate the water for divine purposes.

Next, trace a symbol in the water, of the Creator, that is familiar to you and which is part of your own culture.

Finally, contain this all, by tracing a circle clockwise in the water. By creating a clockwise motion, the forces gather momentum and flow back toward the source of life itself.

DAY 16

A simple consecration of oil

Select and carefully clean a bowl to contain the oil. Pour a small amount of olive oil into it. Olive oil is a connection to the ancient symbol of peace.

Take the bowl of consecrated water that you have already prepared. Dip the first two fingers of the right hand into the water and then shake your fingers three times, so that the water falls into the oil. Using the same two fingers, draw a circle three times into the oil. Leaving your fingers in the oil, call on the insurmountable thought force of the Arch Angel Mikael, (which means "who of us is like unto the Creator?)" Ask this force to consecrate the oil for divine purposes.

DAY 17

A simple consecration of salt

Select and clean a bowl to contain the salt. Pour the salt carefully into the bowl, acknowledging that it represents the physical world in which we live.

Dip the first two fingers of the right hand into your consecrated water and shake three times into the salt. Next dip the first two fingers of the right hand into the consecrated oil and shake three times over the salt.

Using the same two fingers, draw a circle three times clockwise into the salt. Leave your fingers in the salt and call upon the thought force of all life Sandalfon and the Arch Angel who breathes this life into the physical universe, the Arch Angel Uriel (which means The Creator is my Light).

Ask this force to breathe life into and to consecrate the salt for divine purposes.

DAY 18

Candles

Why are candles used across the world in prayer and sacred rituals?

A candle represents the four elements, which is an ancient way of explaining the ever more condensing levels of existence. The flame represents the element of fire; the dimension of the Spirit. Fire is the illustration of the emissive forces of creation and has been given the title of the Father, the Spirit and Fire.

As the candle burns, wax begins to flow downward. This liquid, mutable transformation represents the world of the Soul, the world of water. This is the receptive state of gestation. It has been called the Mother, the Soul and the dimension of Water.

The combination of the flame and liquid creates smoke. This represents the world of Air and the etheric and astral planes.

This has been named the Son, the product of emissive and receptive forces. A new quintessence, that carries thoughts, prayers and dreams into the ether; this is illustrated by the symbolic aspect of Air.

All of this is possible because all these transformative dimensions lay dormant in the solid candle, waiting to be ignited. The Solid candle represents the Earth and physical matter.

It has been named the Daughter, the physical representation of matter and the world in which we live.

When we light a candle, this is a magical and sacred act, connecting us to all the levels of existence and enables us to blend within each moment of transformation.

Creating an altar

The process of creating an altar or prayer table, is an act of sacred concentration. Each object must be placed down with thought and care.

Firstly, place a symbol of the Creator at the head of the table. This signifies our respect for the force of life itself, within which we dwell. A symbol which is part of our culture, even if it is not a religion that we necessarily resonate with, will work best. This is because a symbol that is familiar, is unconsciously imbedded within our consciousness and memory, so the connection is spontaneous.

Place a candle at each of the four corners of the table. Place them down clockwise, starting at the top of the table.

Each candle represents the four elements in itself. They also represent the four dimensions and the four directions, as they are put in place on the table.

The first, at the top left, represents the Spirit and Fire. The next, at the top right, represents the Soul and Water. The candle at the bottom right illustrates the dimension of Air and the etheric and astral planes. The last candle at the bottom left communes with the Earth and physical matter.

Place a small bowl of consecrated water (representing the Soul) under the symbol and then a small bowl of consecrated salt (representing the physical world).

We must always spend time carefully washing our hands, before lighting our candles and setting an altar. Resist the temptation to talk, after the first candle is lit. Silence is a magical moment after candle lighting and creates the space in the world of sound and the Soul. The Soul will then absorb and gestate the sounds of the magical prayers.

What is the true symbolism of the sign of the cross?

The sign of the cross is far more ancient than the Christian idea. It is recognised as the symbol of creation by many of the most ancient ethnic cultures, in diverse regions across the world. The cross itself, was not the object of suffering and death, which has become absorbed into the Western Christian religion. In fact, a crucifixion was generally carried out on a T shaped structure. The cross itself represents the entirety of the Tree of Life. It is made up of six vertical cubes and four horizontal cubes. In three dimensions, there are 22 faces created by each cube. They all have a sound and each are illustrated by one of the 22 Hebrew letters.

The cross represents the structure of creation, the Tree of Life unfolded. Emmanuel, the inheritor of the sacred wisdom of the Initiates and the descendant of the House of David the King and Solomon the Wise, was said to have been "nailed" in sacrifice to the Cross. This symbolises the sacrifice of an Initiate, devoted to the sacred Tree of Life, the ancient cross of wisdom. The nail is the pictorial symbol of the sacred Hebrew letter Vav, this is a letter that represents the great wise sages.

DAY 21
Weekly Review

Let us review the information we have received. Do we now feel that we may take an active part of creation? Little by little, has it become clear that we do not have to be the victim of circumstance and that we have the power to overcome all odds? By using careful methods of cleansing our thoughts, feelings and actions and by working actively, using the age- old knowledge of sacred prayer and ancient wisdom, we can take control of the direction of our lives and rejoice in the endlessly possibilities which surround us?

BLOCK OF LESSONS

True Magic

DAY 22

The true cross

How to trace the cross over the body.

By tracing the symbol of the cross over our bodies, we are consciously communing with the divine forces of creation and life itself.

The sign of the cross is traced by using the forefinger and thumb joined. The forefinger represents our will and the thumb represents the Earth on the human hand. By joining them in a conscious act, we are connecting our spirit and physical body together.

Dip the forefinger and thumb joined fingers into the blessed water.

This is the blessing, the prayer of the sacred cross

Atah (This means "only within and unto thee") It is vital to understand that there are some sounds and words that may only be said in communion and reference to the Creator and the lifeforce. This word has no meaning and no sound in any other dimension and existence, other than our reverent communing within Life.

Malkuth   (the Kingdom)
ve Gevurah (the Power)
ve Gedulah (the Glory)
le Olahm   (all created things dwell within God)
Amen   (so it is and shall be)

Introduce waves of light by using both hands, three times in a wave and then resting on the Ajna chakra.

Simple prayers for your Holy Day

When our Creator saw that the children would perish, because they did not see the Light of Life, the Creator chose the best of the children of Light, so that they might bring the Light of Life to shine before the children of our sacred Earth.

They were called Ishim, because they taught the ignorant and healed the sick. They gathered on the eve of every seventh day, to rejoice with the angels.

We then give thanks for all we have and entrust all we are, and all we will become, to the Creator, within whom we dwell and are inseparable from.

Closing prayer

We thank Thee, Heavenly Creator, for you have put us at the source of the Eternal Life.

The sacred river of Life, which flows from an Eternal source; watering an eternal garden of wonders.

The Tree of Life, mystery of mysteries, growing everlasting branches, for eternal planting. To sink their roots into the stream of Life, from the eternal source.

And thou, my Heavenly Creator, protect these fruits, with flames of eternal light, burning every way.

We then dip our fingers into the blessed water once more and draw the symbol of the cross over us to close the prayers.

Atah, Malkuth, ve Gevurah, ve Gedulah, le Olahm, Amen

We then blow out the candles clockwise from top left to bottom right. We waft the smoke upwards, as our prayers rise to the Divine.

What is the Holy Pentagram?

We often see the pentagram implemented in various rituals and traditions. Especially those who wish to bond with more nature- based religions. Few people remember its origins.

The sages and Initiates have, for many thousands of years, received through devoted meditation and study, sacred names and formulae, that open the sacred gates of the Tree of Life.

Every two thousand years, an Initiate discovers an aspect of the Creator, previously unknown to humanity. Each new aspect has a sacred word, a holy Name of the source of its creation and of the Creator. These Names of the Creator hold unimaginable power; the power to create a universe and eternal dimensions of life. These names have been recorded for us within the Tree of Life itself.

The Holy Pentagram is the sacred name of the Creator which was revealed to the great Initiate Emmanuel and has filtered down to us over the generations.

The Holy Pentagram is made up of five Holy Letters. The first four letters that accumulate the force of life and physical creation are Yad He Vav He and are known as the Tetragrammaton, (this word contains more than entire life's work of knowledge and requires devoted study to begin to understand its power).The fifth letter is the Holy letter Shin, the letter which is the sound of Divine Fire and the ignition of the spirit into matter. Thus, the word "Yad He Shin Vav He", creates the sacred name of the Creator, which has been filtered down to us as" Yah He Sh Va H" or, in the western world, "Jesus". This is why the Initiate, who was named Emmanuel, as we may read the New Testament, told his disciples, only through this Name may you understand our Father. This Sacred Name of the Creator, was not and never was, the name of a human person, but was the sacred name of the Creator, revealed after two thousand years, to the great Initiate, Emmanuel.

Wearing the Holy Pentagram

Now that we have realised the enormity of the pentagram, and the letters with which it is formed, we are better equipped to understand the immense power it encompasses.

As we see, this symbol has been included in many practises and is even used as a jewel or an amulet by those who wish to state their religious pagan beliefs. The same of course may be said of the symbol of the cross.

These symbols have been adopted throughout the generations, but the source, wisdom and power behind them has been watered down and lost in the midst of time.

The pentagram, however, is an extraordinarily powerful symbol. It must be used with respect and reverence. This is more than an arbitrary symbol; it is an immense force of creation and life. If this symbol is worn, then it should always be contained within a circle, as it has the power to command countless invisible entities and forms of life. Without this circle, which represents le Olahm, (all things contained within the Creator and within the force of life itself), the wearer is actually proclaiming themselves to be above the laws of life and greater than the Creator. This can lead to all manner of problems when the protection of the symbol is removed and the wearer exposed for who they are.

How to trace the Holy Pentagram

The Holy Pentagram has been incorporated in many magical rituals and there are many ways of using it to invoke or banish entities.

The ancient wisdom and understanding of this symbol must be the source of years of devoted study.

The Holy Pentagram is traced in this way
The first line is drawn horizontally, right from left. This is the force of life which flows on the Tree of Life from Sephira Chokmah to Sephira Binah. This represents the connection of wisdom and understanding. It is horizontal, because it is balanced and in a perpetual state of equilibrium.

So, the first line represents Divine Wisdom and is illustrated and brought into being with the sound of the letter Holy letter Yad.

The second line is drawn diagonally, in a downward direction, connecting Sephira Binah to Sephira Chesed upon the Tree of Life. This represents that only within absolute, balanced wisdom, may we begin to understand the truth of Love itself, culminated in Sephirah Chesed.

The second line represents Divine Love and is illustrated and given life with the sound of the sacred letter He.

The third line is traced from in an upward, diagonal motion from Sephira Chesed to the topmost sphere of the Tree of Life, Sephira Kether. This line reveals that only through true Wisdom and unconditional Divine Love may we contemplate absolute Truth; the source of all.

The third line is the essence of Truth, the absolute. It is illustrated and called into being by the sound of the Sacred letter Shin.

The fourth line of the Holy Pentagram flows diagonally downward from the highest aspect of the Tree of Life, from Sephira Kether to Sephira Gevurah. Sephira Gevurah is the culmination of all these forces and transforms into Divine Justice itself.

Thus, the fourth line is created by the joining of Wisdom, Divine Love, Absolute Truth and Justice. It is given life by the sound of the Holy Letter Vav.

The final force and the completion of the Holy Pentagram is drawn diagonally upward and connects Sephira Gevurah to Sephirah Chokamh, from whence the force was born. This is the force that illustrates our own human destiny. It represents the possibilities within each human to become the Holy Pentagram and resonate each letter that vibrates within the Children of Light.

The fifth force is a harmonic, the repetition of the letter He, the hidden feminine force which has become unveiled in the physical world in which we live.

Here we have all five letters and the beginnings of the immense wisdom contained within the Holy Pentagram and the Name of the Creator, which was revealed to the great Initiate, Emmanuel.

To be sure, this symbol has been utilised and adapted over many generations. We should take the time to reflect upon its Sacred origins and true meaning.

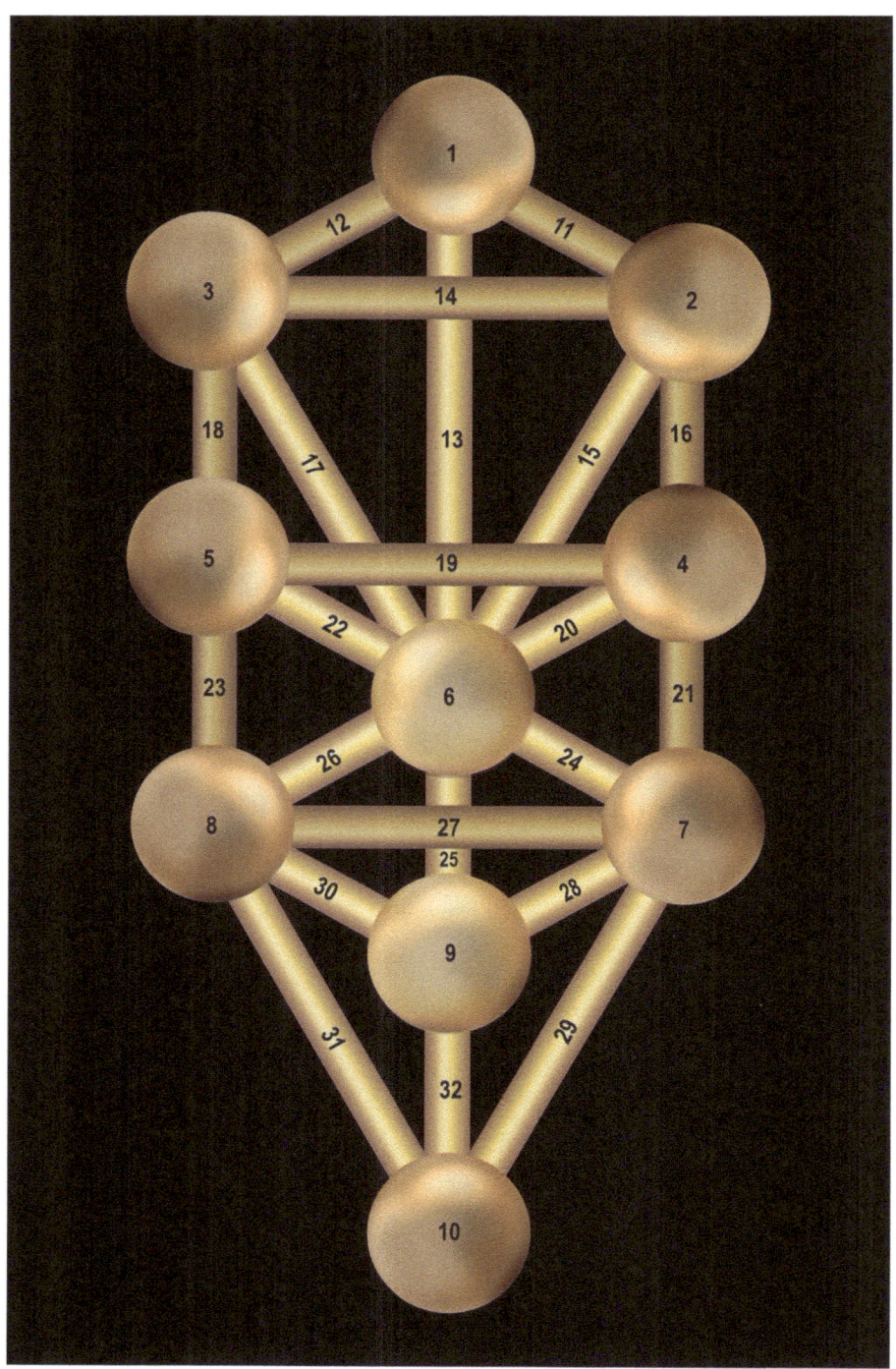

A more in depth understanding of the Tree of Life may be
discovered in the book "The Birth of God" by the same author.

A simple ritual to consecrate our home

We begin by washing our hands and feet in silence and with care. Next, our altar must be set up particularly with this intention in mind. For this consecration, we will need to set down in the centre of the altar, our symbol of the Creator, at the head. Next, our four candles to be lit in a clockwise direction. Under the symbol of the Creator, we set down our consecrated water, our Holy Oil and our blessed salt.

We must also understand that our own thoughts and feelings must be given a spring clean, before expecting any ritual to be effective. A ritual may have a limited result and will certainly work in the short term, but unless we have taken responsibility for our own thoughts and feelings, we cannot expect any kind of sacred results, when our own ingredients are contaminated.

Silence is the most important quality, in the setting up of the altar and the practise of any ritual. The power suspended in silence is unimaginable.

We use the Tree of Life sacred cross prayer, in order to allow us to commune with the highest divine energies.

After saying this prayer, we spend a little time suspended in silence.

We then dip the first two fingers of the right hand, firstly into the water, and shake the water three times into the salt; we repeat this with the oil.

We then draw a circle clockwise into the salt, thus coiling the energies back toward the source of creation itself. We leave our two fingers in the salt.

These are the words to use for this consecration. Remember that all Holy rituals must be voiced with reverence and respect. This is not a magical ritual whereby a magician booms their words and attempts to assert their power. This process is one of listening and vibrating in harmony with entities of purity and wisdom, beyond our comprehension.

As I work this right, these magical implements take life.
I call upon the sacred forces of consecration, and the
messengers flow to me.

This must be said three times over.

The prayer of consecration

Clean shall be the Fire, clean shall be the Water, clean shall be the Air and clean shall be the Earth

Clean are the Sun, the Moon and the Stars

Clean shall be the faithful man and the faithful woman

(n.b this term does not refer to faithfulness to one another, it is a far higher understanding. This term means, faithful unto Truth and to the Divine)

Clean shall be all things created by the Holy Law, whose offspring is the Holy Creation.

The fingers are then removed from the salt and the closing Tree of Life cross is repeated to close the ritual. The candles are left alight on the altar to burn through.

Take the bowl of salt, water and oil and trickle the contents around the perimeters of the house. Draw a line across the threshold and the window sills. Use the contents to trace a Holy Pentagram, with reverence and understanding of all it portrays and close it within a circle, drawn clockwise.

Do this with the first two fingers of the right hand.

Finally, say some quiet words of thanks and invite Holy angelic forces to inhabit your home.

DAY 27

A simple ritual of protection and banishing of evil thoughts and magic

What is the truth of evil that may have been sent your way by the misguided?

Is there any power in this? Can real damage be done?
All thoughts have immense power. All feelings create a semblance of reality. Of course, if you become aware that someone may wish you harm, then your thoughts and feelings quickly gather together and begin to add fuel to the fire.
By carrying out this simple ritual, you will re- discover your own power and certainly, these ancient, simple methods, will do their work of protection. All entities are compelled to abide by the ancient sacred symbols.

However, it is vital to accept that the Holy Law is absolute, it cannot be fooled or swayed. The most important work you can do, is to purify your own thoughts, your own feelings and your own physical actions and way or life. The energy you produce acts as an exact magnet. Always remember this, it matters not, what elaborate rituals you may perform, they may work temporarily, but only your own forcefield will suffice, in truly attracting that which you purport to desire in your own life and within the world in which you live.

Ritual

Follow all the steps as in the earlier prayers and rituals.

For this ritual you will need an empty bowl and in addition to the consecrated water, oil and salt, you will need some powdered hot red pepper.

Red and white represent the Divine forces of masculine and feminine, the emissive and receptive forces. The heat of the pepper, combined with the red, creates a powerful barrier of magical energy. By carrying out this ritual, we take back control of what we allow into our lives.

When our altar has been set and we have carried out the opening Tree of Life sacred cross prayer, we pour equal parts of the consecrated, salt, water and oil mixture, followed by the red pepper.
(Always use an unopened packet and discard anything unused on to the earth, with thanks and do not re use).

Trace a circle clockwise into the mixture and leave the first two fingers of the right hand in the mixture, while you say these words.

As I work this rite, these magical essences take life. I call on the forces of Divine Justice and Power, and these forces embrace me.

Say this three times over, with reverence and respect.
Next, use the same prayer of consecration as used for the consecration of the home.

Close the ritual with the Tree of Life sacred cross prayer and give thanks for this sacred moment. Leave the candles to burn through. Take the bowl of salt and red pepper and use it to draw a line around any openings to the house, using the first two fingers of the right hand.

Pay attention to doorways, window sills, chimney places and mirrors.

Sprinkle some of this mixture under the inner soles of shoes; your shoes and the shoes of others in the home (they do not need to be told about this for it to be effective).

You may use this also in your car or any means of transport.

Use this also to draw a barrier around your beds and also use it to draw a Holy Pentagram on the floor of the head of beds or anywhere else you feel drawn to.

(Remember that even the simple process of making your bed each day, is of great importance. This not only frees you from the world of sleep, but helps you to prepare a place of sanctuary for the coming night).

Finish this by giving thanks and celebrating the freedom you have claimed.

Discard anything left over into the earth with thanks and wash your hands in quietness and calm reverence.

Weekly Review

Is it clear now, that no amount no amount of smudging with sage sticks, or, indeed, any ritual, is effective in the long term, if our thoughts and feelings are in conflict, and we are still attracting unhelpful currents and unwanted entities?

The process of carrying out rituals when accompanied by well - practised, daily habits of cleansing our thoughts, feelings and actions is an immensely empowering and, at the same time, humbling experience. In this way, we learn the immensity of our own existence and the infinite and unseen forces of life within which we live.

BLOCK OF LESSONS

Magic lives within

Live Magically

To truly live a magical life, there is no other route than to prepare, each and every day, the circumstances that will allow powerful magical repercussions. Miracles are created within. Magic exists, all the time, every second of the day, but it is born of our internal life.

Searching for something to save us, looking for the latest guru, depending upon exterior circumstances, or even beseeching a God in the sky, is not the answer.

The only true and sustainable life, and the one that we are compelled to live within, whether we object or not, is the life within which we dwell constantly. This is the life of our thoughts and feelings. It is this reality that creates our perception of reality and it is this life that is the quintessence of true magic.

The first two books in this series give more detailed explanations of the functions of each subtle body. There is an endless amount for us to learn about our own make up.

Higher Nature				
The Spirit	The world of the spirit. The World of light	The element of Fire	The sense of sight	The capacity to Divide
The Soul	The world of the Soul. The world of sound	The element of Water	The sense of Hearing	The capacity to Multiply
The Higher intellect	The world of higher etheric through the world of perfume	The element of Air	The sense of Smell	The capacity to Multiply

Lower Nature				
The Lower mental body	The world of lower thoughts. The etheric planes	The element of Air	The sense of Taste	The capacity to Subtract
The Astral body	The world of lower emotions. The astral planes	The lower element of Water	The sense of Taste	The capacity to Add
The will to survive. Physical body	The physical world	The element of Earth	The sense of Touch	The capaticy to Add

DAY 30

Polarity

All things in creation are made up of a balance of masculine, emissive ingredients and feminine receptive qualities. This is true in every aspect of our beings. Today the subject of transgender people is in the forefront. This is not and never has been a new experience. In many cultures there has been an acceptance of the many different balances of human beings. However, the best way of celebrating the differences between us, is not by annihilating one terminology at the expense of another. Those who truly feel the necessity of physically transforming their bodies, must also understand, that there is an entire world of discovery within the wisdom of how each individual's subtle bodies behave and react. Without understanding the deeper aspects of our beings, true happiness and sustainable balance will never be achieved.

It is more helpful to teach children at an early age about how their different bodies react and allow them to truly learn within themselves, than to "treat" a condition externally. Whatever the choice of an individual evolves into, will always be arrived with a deeper understanding of their entire make up.

DAY 31

Sacred

The sacredness of the sexual forces has, since the dawn of time, been understood. Today, in the world in which we live, their true power is completely diminished by over sexualised imagery. In this way, our world has become ever more banal. We kid ourselves that this is our way of rebelling against restriction, and somehow this asserts our freedom. The result is that very little is left to the imagination. What was once sacred and reserved as the most special exchange between people, has become a hotchpotch of tawdry, tainted and valueless posturing.

To keep a relationship alive and sacred, it is better, always, to truly value all our senses. Study the table of bodies and begin to deeply investigate it. Learn to understand which sense connects to which subtle body.

DAY 32

Enduring relationships

A relationship will endure longer, when more is left to the imagination! Instead of exposing everything on every level, keep some things private and mysterious! Reserve sexual encounters and exchanges for special times and learn to savour these sacred moments of intimacy. Do not ever undervalue the energy that these exchanges release into the atmosphere around you! Take care in preparing for these moments. The more you cherish this power, the more you treat it with reverence and respect, the longer life you give to your relationships.

Respect the truth that no one is a missing part of another. We all are made up of the continual ebb and flow of the two forces, masculine and feminine. We contain all within ourselves and require no one to make us whole. The ancient symbolism of the bride and the bridegroom tells us this. The Bridegroom represents our emissive spirit and the Bride represents our feminine, receptive Soul.

We may share joy and beauty with another, but, above all else, we must rejoice in our whole and perfect being.

DAY 33

Life forms

The Universe within which we live is teaming with life; life of every conceivable possibility. As humans we tend to want to put a shape that we recognise to these life forms; we wish to humanise everything. When we begin to investigate the spirit of life which inhabits a tree, we immediately start to conjure up a magnificent humanoid figure. Our small flowers, for us, are inhabited by tiny human people and the rocks, by gnomes and trolls.

By becoming still and learning to listen to life force within each thing we contemplate, we may begin to truly understand the life force within. We may learn to absorb the energy it releases and the still silent voice it exudes.

DAY 34
Flowers & trees

The voice of flowers and those of the immense trees, is one of subtle light and fragrance. If we take the time to sit peacefully amongst them, we may begin to vibrate within their astonishing colours. We begin to feel our energy change and we may even begin to learn the art of communication with the space and light.

There is no better teacher than the Great Book of Living Nature and no greater spiritual wealth of wisdom than the Sun.

DAY 35

Weekly Review

How do we now feel about the power we have at our fingertips? Do we truly love and respect, even the ground beneath our feet? There is no end to the ways of summoning up true magic, if we care to take the time to greet the world in which we live. This is the world from which there is no escape, our own inner and private world of our thoughts and feelings. What immense possibilities dwell there!

BLOCK OF LESSONS

6

Live selectively

DAY 36

The space between

It is the space between the unseen atoms that dance interminably, which holds the key of true magic. This is the stillness that holds all life in perpetual motion. We may begin to sense this in those sacred moments between each breath we take. We can commune with this infinite space, in the daylight itself and in the darkness between the stars.

When we learn to take our own opinion out of the equation, we truly begin to listen to the space in between reality. The art of invisibility, is the art of stepping out of our personality, so much so, that others often do not even notice us. This can be perfected to such a degree, that we can sit in a room and remain completely unseen by others. It allows us to become part of the wild wood, where we watch animals and leave them undisturbed by our presence.

The art of invisibility, is one of the most precious gifts and the most magical skill of all.

DAY 37

Poisons

It is better to believe and to trust in the integrity of the Higher Nature of each and every human, than to dwell on the ominous "up to no good" "rulers" of the world! Believe, trust and encourage their Higher Nature, for even they have one too!

The more fuel we give to the tales of their evil agenda, the stronger and more likely it is to manifest.

It is more intelligent not to play the game! Take away your fuel and cease to stoke the fire. Concentrate instead upon your own agenda. Become absorbed in the improvement of your own internal world. In this way, you are far more equipped to stand up and be counted. You may be disappointed in people, but you will be in a far better place in yourself. The only way to truly change the world, is for each and every one of us to work away within ourselves! This is how one candle may ignite many.

DAY 38

Recognise poison

Poison exists on so many levels. Learn to use your discerning lower mental body to sniff it out! Learn its taste and its smell! We often think by immersing ourselves in the murky world of social media, where everyone is an armchair expert, on more or less everything that is going on behind the scenes, that we are somehow evoking change. This is a fool's errand and is rife with red herrings!

The first and most important poison to detect and reject is living life vicariously on our phones! Use them, to be sure, but only when truly necessary. The greatest tragedy today is that small square world within which people live!

If we bombard ourselves with information that is distressing, then we are becoming part of that ourselves. So too, is it unwise to post words of wisdom, without taking the time to work on ourselves, with discipline and respect for the ancient techniques of the initiates. This leads to mental imbalance and despondency.

Read the signs

Before putting your trust, your money and yourself into following the latest guru, or the latest trend or into trusting even the most prolific voice, study the story, written in their face. Very often, lurking just beneath the surface, or even in extremely plain sight, is the truth of the state of their inner world.

Learn to look deeply, study their gestures, their nuances, their small signs.
Ask yourself "would I buy a used car from this person!"
Learn to take mere words with a pinch of salt! Then get back to your life, your own daily techniques and practises. That is the only place where your own personal magic and miracles take place.

DAY 40

Two or more

What was the true meaning of the words of Emmanuel, recorded in Gospels "when two or more are gathered in my name, then I am there amongst you?"

This was a lesson in understanding how the subtle bodies work. When we begin to assess how our lower bodies are behaving and reach out for solutions. By simply asking "what can I do, right here and right now, to improve the situation?" we are already using the first body of our higher nature, the Higher Intellect. In this realm dwells the Christ factor, the sacred name YHSVH, the sacred pentagram. The holy name that vibrates within the "Real" and only true aspect of all human beings.

In this way, one or more of our subtle bodies are joined with one of our higher bodies, the Higher Intellect. Here is the source of the Child of the Creator, who dwells in Sephira Tifaret, and is the source of each and every one of us.

DAY 41

Accept time

Very often things get worse before they change. Contemplate the energy that has gone into creating the unfortunate events that are unfolding; resist, with all your might, the temptation to tell and retell again the old story. Resist complaint and dwelling in swamps of despondency. Resist feeling sorry for yourself and vociferating the unfairness of it all. These are the times, when, if you hold on just for a little while, things are about to change for the better. Change they will, for nothing ever remains static. By resisting the temptation to dwell in your misfortune, you are able to tip the balance and create all you wish for. If you stay committed to your techniques and daily practises, physically, emotionally and mentally, this is the time when you can turn events in your favour.

Time is not linear and it does not abide by the rules to which we have become accustomed. A simple trick that we can employ to speed up results which we wish to enjoy, is to "bend" time. This can be done by saying "remember when I was waiting for this to manifest?" " Do you recall when ?"

In this way, the rules are bent and we find ourselves quickly in the position of remembering the events before we had achieved the results. This creates the reality of the achievement, itself.

Weekly Review

   Never slip into the poison of excuse making. When we make excuses and reasons why we cannot carry out simple daily routines and take responsibility for how we choose to see the world in which we live, then we are contributing to all we purport to dislike. Never justify why our situation is not as we would like it to be and then go on to use this as a reason why we cannot make the changes that we know will help us.

Never play the pernicious and poisonous blame game, that stems from an underlying current of self-pity. Never truly voicing our complaint and subtly hinting at the culpability of others! What a cowardly and passive means of stirring up guilt and uncomfortable feelings in our friends and family!

No matter what our situation may be, if we are struggling financially, physically, with illness, disability or with severe pain, we still have an immensity before our eyes and endless tools that we can implement in order to transform how we encounter the world and how we affect other people.

Do we now truly understand our responsibility and accept the challenge?

BLOCK OF LESSONS

Techniques are vital

DAY 43

Keep going!

Nothing takes the place of quietly practising your daily techniques. Genius, on its own, is not enough. Inspiration is not enough! Luck is not enough! Only discipline, endurance and dedicated perseverance can ever have lasting results. Learn from the natural world within which you live. The Great Living Book of nature reveals all, to those who have the respect to listen. Learn from the immense trees; they started life as one small seed. A seed which contained all their extraordinary possibility! All they need is a little time, a little water, a lot of light and lifetimes of endurance and perseverance.

DAY 44
Dust pan and brush

If you are lucky enough to have some stairs or steps, or even if you may borrow some from a friend, this process is extremely useful. By following this technique and putting it into practise from time to time, we can learn the great depths of many things that are troubling us internally.

Take a dust pan and brush (no, a vacuum cleaner will not do!)

Start at the top of the flight of stairs. Before starting, bring all your troubles up into your mind and visualise them all in front of you, sitting on the top step.

Select one thing only, tell the other problems that they must wait their turn!

Visualise that selected problem or unwanted feeling on the step and begin, gradually and systematically to clean it away. As you clean, take a look at it, why do you feel that way? What is the real nature of it, injustice or turmoil? Go on decisively cleaning it away until, by truly understanding it, it has been removed. Ask yourself questions about why you feel troubled. Did you expect better? Did you deserve more? Tell yourself, "that may be so, but I chose to clean away everything that continues to contaminate my home within". Clean away the unwanted, so you may be free and start afresh, without this unpleasant sensation.

Sometimes the problem may persist and you may have to continue your cleaning work on to the next step. Do not move on to choosing another subject to apply to your cleaning process, until the one before has been properly dealt with.

At first you will find yourself vigorously brushing away! By the time you are half way down the flight of stairs, you will find yourself brushing carefully, slowly and even removing tiny fragments of debris with your fingers!

This is the most effective technique to rid yourself and to visit the true depths and real causes of your unwanted feelings.

Even those of us who are unable to physically carry this out, may be able to utilise this process mentally.

DAY 45

Preparing food

We have learned a great deal already about food preparation. It is important to give some time to thinking about the way in which we cook and serve food to others. The process of preparing, cleaning, stirring food, is a magical process.

Learn to stir food in a clockwise direction; this is the magical art of creating a momentum, which flows toward the source of life and to the Creator.

We all instinctively know how it feels to have a plate of food dumped down with aggression in front of us! Equally we all know, deep down, that we wield immense power in doing this to others ourselves! This act has enormous connotations and repercussions! When preparing food with care, even asking for the food to be charged with magical and life- giving elements, we are using an age- old magic. Fairy tales go back to the dawn of time about this power and folklore is full of the belief in the magic of food.

Instead of searching out horror stories of what food may contain, choose what you prepare carefully, cook it with magical intent and serve it with the intention that you wish to create.

DAY 46

Do you expect results to differ from the ingredients you have put into your creation? Learn to think of your own experiences and also the world within which you live, as a simple cooking experiment. We would not put poison into a cake, share it amongst our friends and even our children, or eat it ourselves and expect to survive it, without harm!

Our thoughts, our feelings and certainly our words, have exactly the same cause and effect. How often do we join in with relish, a chance to complain and be incensed with the wrongdoings of the great, unnamed "Them"! How often do we hear ourselves say "They" are up to no good again!

In reality, we have no idea who "They" are! We do better to look within, assess how much of our own inner turmoil is represented in the world outside of us? How kind, how sensible, how generous and responsible have we been internally? Imagine the results in the world, if we all took a stand and equipped ourselves properly in our own internal world, before taking on the task of transforming the world in which we live?

In reality, we have the leaders we so richly deserve!
If we wish to rid ourselves of the world leaders, whom we have allowed to take power, then we can only do so, if we have a viable and sustainable solution, with which to replace them. This work starts internally, with discipline and respect for our own true state of being.

DAY 47

Garbage

Would we go to someone's home with a bin brimming with garbage? Would we storm through the door and tip it all over their floor? Would we then proceed to kick around the decaying and smelly contents?

This is exactly what we do when we use our friends and associates in order to vent our spleen, voice our complaints and try to stir up a reaction. We hope for others to join in and justify our complaint.

We search for safety in numbers!

All the time we are aiding and abetting the very things we wish to transform in our lives. All the time, we are adding fuel to the fire.

If we truly and honestly wish to transform our world, then we have no other choice to reach sustainable change, than to begin, diligently, the work within.

DAY 48
Spiritual Cheating

Progression is natural and inevitable, and not an order! Your progression is your job, alone. It is not effective to spout wise spiritual words and expect to con the great laws, when, in reality, you are unwilling to commit to the inner work that awaits you.

Be selective of the people you interact with on a daily basis! This does not mean you have to be unkind; distance can be imperative in transformation. You can always extend help from a distance later, when you are in a stronger position yourself.

Do not use the idea of reincarnation to judge yourself or others. Your own situation and condition are more than enough to occupy you, without straying into someone else's business! The word "Karma" is not a weapon! You cannot cheat the eternal Laws of Cause and Effect by being spiritually smug, and saying " I am a spiritually evolved being and want no retribution, I am free of judgment!" and then swiftly follow it up with "Karma will sort you out, good and proper" in other words "you'll get what's coming to you, Pal!" The Law of Cause and Effect is exact and responds to your inner thoughts and deepest feelings. It cannot be cheated, bamboozled or soft soaped!

Weekly Review

You belong here on the Earth, you are human, it is a privilege.

You are not a being who does not belong here.

You are not from another planet, no matter how comforting that may be.

Your life, your job and your destiny, is to love this Earth with all your might!

We cannot say we love the Earth and at the same time vow never to reincarnate upon it again!

We cannot say we love the Creator and then try to avoid creation itself!

Value is what we decide.

Learn to love, cherish and value who you are, for that is your only liberation and your only path to achieving the future you desire. This is true magic!

BLOCK OF LESSONS

The Tree of Life

What is the Tree of Life?

The ancient symbol of the Tree of Life, is the most profound and magical source of all knowledge. This is why this symbol can be found in all cultures, right from the dawn of time. The symbol has developed and grown, as humanity's ability to record the divine world of creation has progressed. The illustration of the Tree of Life may be depicted in different ways according to the traditions and psychology of the culture. Some are more imaginative and flamboyant, others simple and concise, some are geometric and mathematical. The Tree of life, no matter from which part of the Earth it has migrated, contains, in condensed form, the entirety of the story of creation and of the infinite life forms it supports.

The Sephirotic Tree of Life

The Sephirotic Tree of Life contains within it, the mathematical keys of creation. To study the Tree of Life is to embark upon a journey of discovery; a journey that has many beginnings, but one that can never end.

To study the Tree of Life is a commitment to listening. It is a commitment to stillness, the putting aside of our opinions and to learning to listen at an acute and previously undiscovered level.

The first process is to study the symbol, begin to be familiar with names recorded upon it. These words have been received, over thousands of years, by the great Initiates. The letters and numbers which form them are precise and reveal worlds within worlds of life and creation.

DAY 52

Memory

Do not try to memorise the words and dimensions of the Tree of Life. The knowledge is too vast to contain within your head! It is by beginning to read them, by beginning to repeat them, that they begin to become absorbed into your very being. If you forget something, just let it go, in the knowledge that it is within the Tree of Life that you have your existence. The words and the wisdom exist eternally and they will visit you once more.

These words are true sacred magic. Some of them shall never be spoken in this dimension. The only way to truly understand them, is to hear them, in silence of your soul.

Ancient Wisdom

Genesis tells us that the Tree of Life grew in garden of Eden

Each aspect, sphere or Sephira of the Tree of life contains an endless holographic universe of Sephirotic Trees. The Garden of Eden is a state of existence flourishing eternally within Sephira Chesed. This is a sacred word, which expresses constant glory and love of the Creator, within which we dwell. The age- old story of humanity within the Garden of Eden, tells us of the first formation of humanity, Adman Kadmon, the King. This word is made of the ancient words for Red, Earth and Breath. It tells us that the first concept of the human state was formed from the red, life giving frequencies, and the breath of existence itself. The receptive, feminine aspect of humanity was formed from "the rib" of Adman. This "rib" originated from the word "lulav" , the palm branch, the spinal cord, which would later enable humanity to walk upright upon the Earth. The Tree of the Knowledge of Good and Evil about which the serpent coiled, is a whole subject of a lifetime's study.

The Tree of Life is also the Tree Knowledge; the wisdom of truly understanding the dark and the light, the entirety of the laws of cause and effect.

In order to begin living within the physical world, humanity had to eat of the apple, the fruit of knowledge, to understand the process of life and death and rebirth.

Revelations

The scriptures record, in Revelations by St John the Divine, that the Tree of Life bares twelve manner of fruit, and these fruits are for the healing of the nations.

This tells us all, that to enter into the great halls of learning, to begin to study the Tree of Life, to learn to set aside our own subjected opinions, is the key to the transformation of humanity and the Earth upon which we live.

The complete Tree of Life has twelve Sephirot, within these lie our entire eternal beings and the whole of Creation.

DAY 55

Magic and Miracles

The words and formulae recorded within the Tree of Life are the true keys of magical and miraculous creation. We cannot begin to access them, or begin to become adept at using them, or even speaking them correctly, unless we have committed to honesty within our own inner worlds. Each word, even within our daily conversation, vibrates with hidden reverberations of the real truth of our integrity and the real state of our being.

To study the Tree of Life, is to be always under the spotlight! It is as though we are exposed eternally, for exactly who and what we are!

There is nowhere to go and nowhere to hide! So, we decide to embrace honesty, first and foremost, never to deny the small, nuances that writhe deep within, when we, deep down know, that we haven't truly been all that we had hoped. And that is the key to studying the sacred Tree of Life. Always be ready to fall on your face, laugh at your own absurdity, the way we try to exonerate and kid ourselves, and then, get up, carry on, once again!

DAY 56

Accept miracles

The creation of miracles starts in the minute world beneath our feet. The more we search out, love and respect the miraculous world of creation, the vast impossibility of it all, the more that are able to watch miracles unfold. To deny the miraculous is to deny life itself!

The more we value our ability to breathe, for our hearts to beat, the more we learn to listen to the myriad breath and countless heartbeats that vibrate around the Earth, the more we become capable of creating the miraculous.

Start each morning by calling upon miracles; vow to commit yourself to accepting the tiniest of miracles. This is the pathway toward the momentous; this is the road to the creation of miracles on a grand scale!

DAY 57
Weekly Review

Do we now know that we are privileged, beyond comprehension, to be alive; to experience a physical life. We are blessed to have an abundance of ways to experience the wondrous life of this extraordinary planet. Most of us have the gift of all five senses. Some of us have only some of these wondrous gifts. All of us are able to absorb and experience the incredible force of life in myriad ways. With these gifts, we may, not only immerse ourselves in the magnificent life of our planet, but we may also learn to use these senses to commune and experience higher realms of existence.

This is the devotion to true magic and the path toward the miraculous.

BLOCK OF LESSONS

The only sane path!

Internal Work

So, what is internal work? Why is it so important that we take on this task? True internal work, is the route toward balance and peace. We cannot expect to create a peaceful world if we have not tackled our own internal landscape. Internal work begins with learning the functions of all the different aspects, our subtle bodies, and how they interact with each other. The first two books in this series have investigated this vast subject a little.

Of course, meditation is extremely beneficial, but, this alone, is not enough. Inner work, tracking the reaction of our lower nature and using simple daily techniques helps us to begin to create more balance and peace in our inner world of thoughts and feelings.

The most important thing to accept, is that the lower bodies never change and never give up their attempt to rule the roost! Just as we think we have made progress, just when we have congratulated ourselves on a minor success, in reacting as we would wish in a difficult or testing situation, only seconds later, there we are, ranting and raving, howling out in pain, once again!

This is normal! The lower astral body is destined to forever demand and to say, "I want!". It cares not what it gets, so long as it can add up! That is its function! The lower mental body, the lower thoughts, will always subtract, always acknowledge that the emotional body did not get what it wanted! That is its function!

All we can do, is to search a little higher for our solutions, look beyond and take, just a few seconds to decide what is the best route to take. In this work, a few brief seconds of time are our eternal ally.

DAY 59
Foolhardy positivity

Try to avoid the fashion of "Positive" thinking. This is bound to fail, in reality. Real life has many shades and many colours, it is full of every nuance of emotion. To constantly strain to react positively, under any circumstance, is doomed from the start! It is not natural to deny the reality of the lower nature or to force ourselves to only think positively. This will inevitably lead to feelings of failure and discontent. Neither is it sensible to use forgiveness, of ourselves, or others, in order to exonerate bad behaviour.

The way forward is to acknowledge our true feelings, accept that they have every reason to be heard. When we break our own rules of desired behaviour, then we must hold our hands up to the fault. We may forgive ourselves and others, but that does not mean that the crime was acceptable or that no repercussions will follow! One of the most important things to understand is that we must apologise, to others and to the unseen world within which we live; and never, ever apologise with a "but"! This is a feeble attempt to conceal the truth and to exonerate our behaviour due to circumstance!

Apologise with decency, from the heart and then go about the business of making reparation and trying to live better in the future. Use the daily techniques and go about creating stability once again.

The Swing of the Pendulum

We must not ignore the laws of nature. We cannot expect a high, without the natural swing of the pendulum, in the other direction. That is natural and a physical law.

Today a great deal is spoken about elevating your vibration, but what, in reality, does this truly mean? It is true that the vibration of the energetic field around is created by your thoughts and feelings. It is also true that this has a magnetic pull, and that it draws toward its experiences that match its vibration.

The only thing that we can, in reality and sensibility, attempt, is to regulate the violent swing of our internal pendulum of thoughts and feelings.
It is wondrous to experience elevated and inspired moments.
It is the most glorious of human experience. So, when we are visited by these exhilarating times, it is advisable to come back to earth gradually, in order to avoid a swing of the pendulum, that will hurtle off too far in the other direction.

So how do we do this? Does it mean that we must live a mediocre or humdrum life? Of course not!

By daily practise, we may gradually and cautiously, little by little, achieve a balance and peaceful happiness, that creates a slightly higher vibration in our magnetic field. The swing of the pendulum, gradually becomes tamed, little by little. When we feel exceptionally elevated, give thanks and then pull it back down just a little, so our inner pendulum will swing less in the opposite direction. When we feel low or unhappy, acknowledge it, let it have its voice, and then, we must go about our daily techniques and use them to pull the swing back, once more. In this way, our place of natural balance becomes more easily regulated and sets itself a new position, where our place of balance is at a higher frequency than it was in the past.

DAY 61

Useful technique to overcome addiction

We have in the previous books investigated a little the subject of addiction; we have already learned a little about the nature of drugs and alcohol and other forms of addiction. They all differ and have different effects on the different bodies of lower nature. One thing is for sure, whatever the substance, the deep wish and desired outcome from taking it, is to achieve some kind of liberation and often is an attempt to experience a higher experience of existence. We must learn to rid ourselves of the childish idea that addiction is a moral issue. It is simply bound, as all things are, by the laws of cause and effect. These laws are exact, they cannot be hoodwinked!

The best way of attempting to overcome an addiction is, firstly, leave it alone! Do not give it any more of your time and cease empowering it by furiously fuelling with thoughts of how you must overcome it! Do not expect it to diminish in that way, it has ruled the roost for a while, it will not give up its hold so easily. Next, really spend time every day, whether you are still taking the substance or not, really getting to know the "real" you. Learn about your higher nature. Imagine that very best, most true and most vibrant "real" you that you can conjure up; say hello to that person, draw closer to your very best friend.

You will find this is a natural process toward overcoming an addiction, without quite so much difficulty.

Step 2 Overcoming Addiction

When you have really created a clear and strong image of the "real" you, ask for the help of your very best friend in becoming closer to that version of yourself. Still do not make a concerted attempt to stop the addiction. Leave it alone and do not give it any of your thoughts at all. Whether you take the substance or not, is not important.

When you are feeling closer to the "real" you, then the next step is to mentally choose the image of any everyday object. The instant this object comes into your mind, you must stick with that choice. Do not change the object for something else!

Now, do not think of that object!

You will find that the object just will not go away! It will constantly invade your thoughts! Each time you think of your object, then do something that hurts you just a little. Dig your fingernails into your skin, for instance. Put a rubber band around your wrist and flick it, so that it stings; anything at all, that gives you a little discomfort.

Play this game for a few days and then start to try to consciously not think about the object.

When you are able to reject the object, or it ceases to appear in your thoughts at all, or very seldom. Then you are ready to tackle the substance you wish to stop taking; this is because, by now, you have become used to a little discomfort. Now you are ready to replace the object with the image of the substance and its hold over you, that you wish to overcome. Do the same thing, each time you think about it, snap the rubber band, or dig your fingernails into your skin, cause yourself a little discomfort. This is the time to physically stop taking the substance. You will have become used to the discomfort that this process of giving up a substance will bring. Also, by this time, you will have naturally reduced the amount you have been taking.

Step 3 Overcoming addiction

Of course, it is natural that the lower bodies will require something to replace the substance that you have rejected. The good news is, that the lower astral body of feelings, which is obliged and compelled to add up, will accept anything at all it is given, just so long as it may fulfil its natural function. You have the right to choose what you give it! We have already in previous books discovered that both the lower astral body of lower emotion and its counter -part, the lower etheric body, of lower thoughts, are both connected to the sense of taste. This is why it is easy to replace an addiction with eating something. This, in itself can cause additional problems, in every sense of the word! The most effective and quickest way to fill the gap, is to use your tools of breath. Each time you think of the substance, or feel its need, replace it with three huge breaths of sunlight. Daylight, even if the sun is obscured, is perfect. The light of a candle, or even electric light, is still a physical source of light. Really concentrate on three huge breaths of light, hold in each breath for a little longer than is comfortable. Breathe in the light for all you are worth, hold the breath, let it do its work, then breathe out slowly. Do not take more than three breaths at a time. If you need more than that, allow yourself a few minutes pause before repeating the process.

By applying these three steps, you will find it easier to overcome an addiction; never make the mistake that you have conquered it! It is always there, somewhere lurking in the depths, but just pat it on the head, give it a little light to placate it and allow it to slumber peacefully.

Weekly Review

How far have we come? Where do we go from here? Do we now have a deeper understanding and a more reasonable acceptance of the highs and lows of life? Do we choose to set our inner pendulum at more manageable frequency? Is it better to live a life of peace and balance? May we use this inner work to truly care about the world in which we live? Shall we make a decision to continue this inner work and to embrace reality?

When we stumble or feel overwhelmed, then it is time to take a well -earned holiday! This is so easily achieved. Stop telling yourself you are taking a break or having "time out, as this implies that there is something unpleasant, to which you must return.

Simply, find something that you enjoy, to eat or drink, or read or listen to. Go away! Find a spot to relax in and say to yourself "I am on holiday!" Really savour these few minutes, for all they are worth. Feel the freedom of being on holiday.

You will even be surprised how others react to this unspoken message and leave you alone for a while, in peace!

You can go on holiday every day!

BLOCK OF LESSONS

The vast world of colour

DAY 65
Colour

The world of colour is so vast, it is immeasurable. There are so many hues and shades! None of us experience colour in quite the same way. Some of us see very little of the colour that blesses so many others. Within the world of colour dwells an immensity of wisdom. We have, unfolding before us, every day an infinite display of life. The more we look deeply into a colour, especially if it is the colour of a flower, the more vibrant and extraordinary it becomes. When we spend time immersing ourselves in the colours of plants, we are even able to observe them vibrating with the life force and displaying depths of colour, that seem so very much brighter than we had ever experienced before.

The first three colours, we call primary, because when we try to replicate them, we have discovered that they exist entirely alone and cannot be created by mixing other colours. If we learn a little about the sacred Tree of Life, we may discover that it is not a flat image. It is a structure; the structure of the entirety of creation. In three dimensions, we may see that the three columns of the Tree of Life lead to the topmost world; the world of Atziluth. This is the absolute world of all life, from whence all life flows. This world is the tetrahedron; the lines of power that flow from its pinnacle, are the three primal colours of life itself. These are red, blue and yellow. These three forces create the tetrahedron, which has four surfaces, these are the four secondary colours, that are a blending of the original three colour forces. This combination of three pure forces and of the four surfaces that they create, is the possibility for the world of physical colour to be born. This is the creation of the prism, that receives pure white light and transforms it into the seven light spirits of our own physical world.

DAY 66
The Life Force

Red is the first colour and the force of life itself. So much may be said about colour red. When we commune with a plant that has bloomed and displays its red flowers, if we are still and listen, we may learn the immense force and power, captured within its petals. If we show a little love and respect and give some of our good thoughts to the plant, we may borrow some of its energy and reinvigorate our own physical being. By visualising the colour entering our body and illuminating us, as we breathe in and hold in the red frequency, we can actively overcome tiredness and recover more quickly from an illness. We may use these valuable plants, provided we act with respect, to rise out of mental exhaustion, depression and illness.

DAY 67

Blue

So much may be learned about the blue hues and shades. This has long been associated with royal blood. Blue is the frequency of the Universal Soul. The immortal feminine force, that has, since the dawn of time, been recognised as the Eternal Mother. Blue illustrates the female aspect of the Creator and the source of true, unconditional love.

When we seek out blue flowers, we may begin to learn, through consciously breathing in and immersing ourselves in myriad hues of blue, how to make the first tentative steps into the world of the Divine Soul; the womb of creation. Our birthplace, our home.

DAY 68

Yellow

Yellow is the vibrant frequency of the Higher Intellect. The frequency of yellow uplifts the thoughts of humanity. By working with the yellow flowers, we are able to retain our place within our own Higher Intellect and commune with the dimensions of Higher Thought; the source of all inspiration and imagination; this is the colour of the centrifugal force of the Tree of Life. Yellows and golds; the frequency of the Child of the Creator. When we breathe this in, it elevates our thoughts and we are able to commune with our own "real" self.

Green

Oh, the immensity of Green! Created by the light frequency of Blue, the sacred purity of the Soul, fusing and merging with vibrant Yellow, the Highest dimensions of Intellect. Is it any wonder that our own dear Earth is overflowing with every hue and shade of Green? The colour of Mother Nature herself? How much health and strength we can absorb, by dwelling in the richness of Green all about us? Green is the colour of endurance and of victory!

DAY 70

Orange

   Made up of the Red life force and the Yellow intelligence. Within orange flowers, dwells the voice of health and healing. The rich frequency of Orange, calls out to us, entreating us to imbibe of its wealth and life. The bursting Red life force and the Vibrant Intelligence of Yellow, living in harmony in this sacred frequency. Here we have a constant source, where we may go, to regain our health and sustain recovery.

DAY 71

Weekly Review

Let us use this day to truly appreciate the wealth of colour with which we are blessed. Even if our vision of colour is limited, we may still try our best to hold on to the frequency that we are able to see. We must realise that, the more we search out colour, the more we hold it sacred and the more we listen to the voice of flowers and trees, the greater our understanding, health and joy will become. Colours are there to sustain us and to teach us how to retain happiness.

BLOCK OF LESSONS

So Much More Colour!

Violet

Violets and purples were revered by our forefathers. Only the echelons of society had the right to dress in these hues. Within violets and purples, dwell the entwined frequencies of the Spirit of Life and The Divine Soul. The Bridegroom and the Bride, The Father and Mother of Creation. Red and Blue the sacred source of Creation. By beginning to truly look deeply into the petals of purple and violet flowers, we are able to touch upon the greatest secrets of creation. The gentler, violet, tempered by the pure white frequency of light, teaches us the art of kindness. A whole world of lessons is held within the petals of these hues.

DAY 73
Indigo

The depths of the colour Indigo, reverberate with ancient wisdom. Here are the depths of Sephira Binah, the female face of life and the womb of creation itself. This is the frequency of Contemplation. It is rare indeed, to be lucky enough to find a flower that has been able to truly create this colour. But when we do find one, then we must stop and take the time to absorb its rarity.

DAY 74

Brown

The richness of the Earth, that has an immense and ever-changing hue. The colour of the Sacred Earth itself. Browns. of every description, tell us the story of transformation and the message of our sacred planet. The story of the constant replenishment of the earth, a continual process of the seasons, the ebb and flow of life, are held within the colour Brown.

DAY 75

Pink and tempered colours

We are surrounded by a rich variety of pink flowers, petals that are fused with red and white. The blend of the red life force and the quietude of pure white. Plants that produce flowers with tempered colours can bestow upon us a feeling of gentleness, kindness and peace. When we look deeply into their petals, we see an amazing culmination of light work, of the magic of transformation. We need look no further for messages of kindness and tranquillity; it is up to us to make the most of their beauty and the emanations that bless us so unconditionally.

Black and White

Nothing in our world can truly be said to be Black or White. Everything is a subtle merging of shades. True Black has depths beyond our comprehension, and has its source way before the creation of the Sephirotic Tree of Life. Black is the primal, receptive state of non- existence. It takes many lifetimes to truly understand the depths and magnificence of Black.

White is the purest state of being; it emanates from the first burst of life itself. Within white light, dwells the promise of an endless light spectrum, of countless hues of colour. A brief touch of white within the petal of a flower changes completely the message it conveys to us.

The subject of Black and White is endless and opens the door to mysteries, beyond belief.

DAY 77

Avoid Clashing!

Magenta is a formidable colour. It is the meeting of the visible light spectrum. Infra- red and Ultra Blue meet when the light spectrum is arced. This meeting place creates a colour frequency that is unique and exceptional. We only have to contemplate it for a short time, to begin to unfold the vastness it contains.
This colour gives us a valuable lesson. These two poles seem so different, but when they meet, they create something of intense and unique beauty.

Each and every one of us has their own colours. Some are even able to detect the colour of the auric field that surrounds a person. This aura is the culmination of the energy released by the individual, through the etheric bodies. This energy is made up of the thoughts and feelings and the natural tendencies of the person. These colours are magnificent, but we must take care to abide by the law of colour. All colours are fabulous on their own, but sometimes an unfortunate choice of merging with another colour can create a terrible clash! We must learn which of our human colours blend and match with others and create harmonious hues.

Two people may vibrate with glorious colour, but the colours do not combine, their frequency clashes, the relationship between them does not combine in harmony. The hues are not compatible.

We must accept, that there are some colours that are so powerful, that they cannot merge successfully, and must be allowed to shine alone.

Weekly Review

So, we have learned a little about the extraordinary world of colour; a world that reveals itself endlessly each and every day.

By using all this knowledge and by truly accepting to learn about our own internal world, we are setting about a work of great importance.

It is said that the Messiah rose from the dead, and that he rose in his Body of Glory. The true meaning of the term Body of Glory, is not the physical body, nor the aura, and, not even, the many etheric bodies. This body, is a body that is created, little by little. It is quite separate from the other parts of us. The Body of Glory is a body of wondrous and shining intensity, built by the emanations of every effort, success and burst of joy that we encounter during our lifetime. This body is immortal, and indestructible. The great Initiates have perfected this. When they die in the physical world, their Body of Glory remains forever in the emotional, astral dimensions of the Earth, for all to remember. These are the Ishim, the glorious, the golden ones, whose Body of Glory remains eternally, to guide and encourage humanity.

BLOCK OF LESSONS

12

Angelic Forces and communing with them daily

Monday

So much has been written about angels. What are they, and how do they bless our lives?

The names of some of the Arch Angels have remained in the consciousness of humanity, but little of the true immeasurable and infinite force of which they are made, is really understood. The Arch Angels are immense forces of pure thought, that travel throughout eternity, in the constant creation of reality, in every dimension. They are way beyond our human experience. Their frequency is far higher and far more formidable than us. But divinities made of light and thought frequencies, that vibrate at a rate more akin to ours, also exist. These are the beings that some of us are sometimes consciously blessed by.

Ancient manuscripts have taught us, however, how to commune with the magnificent angelic sources. There are certain days and times, when it is easier for human beings to open themselves to these vast Angelic realms. There are many different traditions and different opinions as to which angelic force is to be focussed upon on which day. The truth is, these are monumental and immeasurable forces of thought, that we, as humans cannot even begin to fathom. To reduce the comprehension of angelic forces to our own opinion and agenda is a great misunderstanding. These days of communion, are simply for us to make our own tentative steps toward forces that are also a permanent part of the many dimensions of life.

Recorded here some of the most ancient communions recorded in long forgotten manuscripts.

Monday is the morning to make our communion with the Angelic force of Life, the vast and unfathomable force called Sandalfon. As we carry out our morning practises, breathe in consciously the life force and begin to feel the never- ending ebb and flow, the tides of light and life.

Midday is an important moment, the time to stop and take stock of where we are. Now is the time to acknowledge a new force of thought. Monday afternoon is the moment for us to open ourselves up to angelic force of Work, the emanations of Arch Angle Haniel; this name means, in the simplest terms, The Grace of God. The voice of this force is said to be heard in the humming of the bee, without whom, the planet would not survive.

DAY 80

Tuesday

Tuesday morning is our opportunity to commune with the immense force of joy, breathed into the universe by the Arch Angel Raphael. This word means "the Healing of God". It is said that when we appeal to this unconquerable life force of joy, that our case will be pleaded incessantly, on our behalf, until we have received a "yes"! We must hold fast to joy and learn to cultivate its quintessence.

At midday on Tuesday, we may temper this exuberance, by communing with the Arch Angel of Peace, the Arch Angel Shamiel, "The Peace of God". The silent angelic force of peace, who sings within the word Shalom, "Peace be with you". This word is made of the three Holy Mother letters and held together in perfect harmony and balance, by the sacred letter Lamed, the force of perfect equilibrium.

DAY 81

Wednesday

Wednesday morning is the time for us to commune with the vast and unfathomable force of the power of creation and the unending flow of life and rebirth. This is heralded by the Arch Angel Gavriel, the word that means "The Power of God" This is our moment to spend in awe of the extraordinary abundance within which we live.

At midday we may pause and feel the change in the air and celebrate the overwhelming force of the Sun and of Daylight. This is heralded by the magnificence of the Arch Angel Mikael. This word is a question "Which of us is truly like unto God?" By communing with the sun, we may begin to understand a whisper of the Creator and the Light of Life.

DAY 82

Thursday

On Thursday morning we may make a delicious communion with the Arch Angel of Water, the Arch Angel Tzaphkiel. This word means, in the simplest terms, "The Contemplation of God". This is our moment to wash in consecrated and blessed water; to cleanse and contemplate. To become still and to listen.

At midday, we feel the tides of water bringing true and unconditional love to our shore. The Arch Angel Tzadkiel, which means "The Justice and Righteousness of God", washes over the physical world. By pausing and making our communion, we may begin to understand true, undemanding and generous love.

DAY 83

Friday

Friday morning is the herald of our timeless days of prayer. It is said that the Angel of Air shall bring them and that every eye shall see them. Ariel, which means "The Lion of God", inhabits the very air we breathe. This is key of life within the physical world. The first breath, heralds our life here, and the last breath we take, signals our transition into worlds beyond.

At midday, the Arch Angel of Wisdom holds open the gates to the holy Days of Prayer. The Ach Angel Raziel, which means "The Wisdom of God", is the gatekeeper of the Holy days. We gather together with all the angelic forces to celebrate our Creator.

Saturday

Earthly Mother

The morning of Saturday is the sacred time to cherish the Earthly Mother. Take the time to find a quiet spot and listen, with your ear to earth itself. If you are truly still, you may hear her heart beating.

The Earth and also our role, is to transform and regenerate. An ancient prayer and communion with the earth, is practised in this way. If you wish to rid yourself of unwanted feelings and undesirable energy, then dig the first two fingers of your right hand into some earth. The following words act in a circular motion, that gives to earth, with a blessing and a request to use the energy as compost, in order to create new and pristine growth.

If you are tired and need a burst of energy, then dig the receptive, first two fingers of the left hand, into the earth, instead.

Whisper these words to the Earthly Mother three times over.

Taro Tora Rota, Ta rota, Ro taro

Heavenly Father

At midday on Saturday, the ancient manuscripts have recorded that we have the blessed moment of communing with the light of life itself. It is written, search first the Kingdom of Light and all shall be given unto you. These words hold a treasury of ancient wisdom. Search within physical light, the living spirit of creation, and the voice of the Heavenly Father. This is to embark upon a journey of discovery, An endless source of joy and the key to life itself.

Weekly Review Sunday

On Sunday morning, we may join within the emanations of the Arch Angel Uriel, the Angelic force of the Earth; this beautiful word which means "The Creator is my Light" An ancient rhyme tells us

"He gathers the prayers wherever he stands and they turn into flowers, within his hands"

At midday, we must pause and take the time to commune with Arch Angel of Eternal Life. The Arch Angel Phaniel, The Eternity of God". Within this name is concealed the transition between life, death and rebirth. We see eternal circles and the eternal reverberation of the song of life.

And so, we have learned the way of the ancient Initiates. We have learned to keep our communions, so that the light of life may burn as a constant flame within us.

It is said, that there are one thousand angels who care for the well -being of every single human being. As we learn to dwell within the myriad divine forces of life, we begin to feel the closeness of these beings and know that we are never abandoned and never alone.

BLOCK OF LESSONS

Planetary Forces

The ancient wisdom of how we commune with cosmos has long been recorded. This is the way our forefathers began to translate into daily ritual, their innate feelings of dwelling within a living universe. In many countries, this knowledge is written into the very days of the week.
The planetary forces emit and recede and take their turn throughout each day, and throughout each hour. Should we plot this down on a graph, we would see wave like forces that ebb and flow perpetually.
This is the simple, daily pattern.

Monday

This is the day when we may commune with the force of the Moon, the receptive, feminine force. That silver quintessence that illuminates the darkness. The word in both English and in French reveals this to us, Monday and also Lundi, from the word for the moon La Lune.

DAY 87

Tuesday

Tuesday is the day of the week when we have the opportunity to commune with the vast planetary force of Mars. This is the fiery, red force of life, that bursts out wherever we care to look. In French it is clearly recorded as Mardi, the day of Mars.
The angelic force of joy, heralds this magnificent abundance.
The enormous force of this day, is tempered by our communion with Angel of Peace.

Wednesday

Wednesday is our day to commune with the planetary force of Mercury. It is our moment to choose clear communication and wisdom. This is the force which governs the Initiates. The symbol of this planet expresses the masculine and feminine forces in harmony upon the Earth. The wings on the ankles of the ancient god Mercury, shows us the ability of even our most base nature, having the promise of flying to the heavens.

The French word for Wednesday is Mercredi, the day of Mercury. So much is concealed within our daily lives and the words we use, without thinking of their hidden depths!

DAY 89

Thursday

Thursday is the day or time to make our communions with the planetary force of Jupiter, this is the force of true, unconditional justice. The force of divine, true justice and righteousness, flows throughout this day. By taking time to commune with water in silence and by sending out our own messengers of love, far and wide, we are able to absorb the immense and eternal force of Jupiter.

The French word for Thursday, is Jeudi, the day of Jupiter.

DAY 90

Friday

Friday is our day to designate to the planetary force of Venus, the planet of divine love; the great, feminine force of creation. We can see this clearly in the French word for Friday, Vendredi, the day of Venus.

This is the day of truth and wisdom, when we gather together with all the angelic forces, to give thanks for creation and to herald in our special Holy days.

DAY 91

Saturday

Saturday is our time to commune with the planetary force of Saturn, the cold and silent place of internal contemplation. This is the force of wisdom, but more accurately, of understanding. Wisdom is gleaned from all we learned from the past; understanding, contains all the ingredients for the creation of the future.

Both the English and the French word have retained their connection to the planet Saturn; Saturday and Samedi, both recall this knowledge.

Weekly Review

Sunday is the day of the celebration of the Sun, the source of life on our planet and the quintessence of the light of the Creator. This is written within the word Sunday and there is also a reminder in the French word Dimanche, the day of the Creator. Let us now realise that we have immense resources before us. We can combine our understanding of the ebb and flow of planetary forces and the vast angelic dimensions with which we may commune. In this way, we can pick and choose the best environment and the best times and days of the week, to have meetings or to communicate with our friends effectively.
How endlessly may we entwine all these lessons? Our daily techniques. Our cleaning practises? The ebb and flow and pendulum swing? Communing with colours? The angelic force of the day and of the night? How rich and abundant are the endless methods and techniques, that are ours to master.

Why not find a small area, a little piece of land that is struggling? Decide to carry out your experiment. Take care to walk across it once or twice a day, if you can. Focus your kindness and love upon it, even if you are physically unable to walk upon it. Make this small spot your very own. Call upon all the wonderous forces that you have learned about. Look out for the tiniest signs of transformation. Call upon the grass, the plants, the animals and divine entities to inhabit it and call it back to life. With patience, dedication and time, you see a wondrous transformation, before your very eyes and you will have done something worthwhile with your life, here upon the earth.

And so, we have reached the end of our little voyage of discovery, contained within our three small books, and we are ready to embark upon something new.

Have we now truly understood and accepted that we all have a vital role to play? Have we committed to practising, each and every day, small techniques that make such grand differences to the world that we pass through, so very briefly?

Have we learned that true magic and miracles exist wherever we look and that they reveal themselves, over and over again, to all of us who search them out and who decide to create them?

Do we vow to care, even for the footsteps we leave behind us?

Do we accept our responsibility?

Humanity is not so much waking up, as growing up.

Thank you for the time you have taken within these pages.

Thank you from the Treasury of Ancient Wisdom

My Notes & Observations

Lightning Source UK Ltd.
Milton Keynes UK
UKHW021014281221
396274UK00006B/88